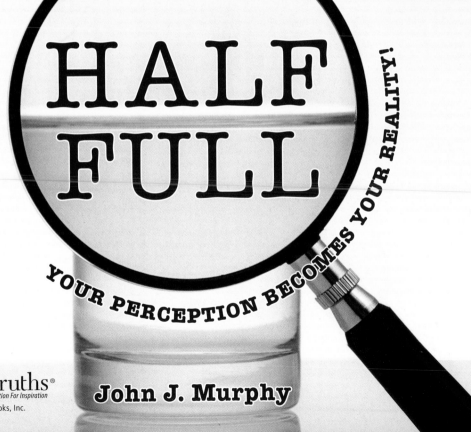

HALF FULL

FULL

YOUR PERCEPTION BECOMES YOUR REALITY!

simple truths®
Your Destination For Inspiration
n imprint of Sourcebooks, Inc.

John J. Murphy

Editing by: Alice Patenaude

Cover and internal design by: Kristi McKay

Photo Credits:

Cover: front, Cosmo Condina/Getty Images; back, DaveBolton/Thinkstock

Internals: page 1, Cosmo Condina/Getty Images; pages 4–5, Zack C/Shutterstock; page 6, Cranach/Shutterstock; page 8, Lalith_Herath/Thinkstock; page 11, Photography by Bobi/Getty Images; page 12, Denis Vrublevski/Shutterstock; page 13, viviamo/Shutterstock; page 14, anhong/Thinkstock; page 16, Laurence Mouton/Getty Images; page 17, Apostrophe/Shutterstock, hudiemm/Getty images; pages 18–19, FotoYakov/Shutterstock; page 20, ouh_desire/Thinkstock, Christin Gasner/Shutterstock, Claus Christensen/Getty Images; page 23, diego cervo/Thinkstock; pages 24–25, Antonio V. Oquias/Shutterstock; page 26, Oleg Mirza/Thinkstock; pages 28–29, kesipun/Shutterstock; page 30, monkeybusinessimages/Thinkstock; pages 32, Kjpargeter/Shutterstock; page 33, Sascha Burkard/Shutterstock; pages 34–35, Terry J Alcorn/Getty Images; pages 38–39, Ifistand/Thinkstock; page 40, Pgiam/Getty images; page 42, da-vooda/Thinkstock; page 43, horiyan/Thinkstock; pages 46–47, Dudarev Mikhail/Shutterstock; page 48, Vstock LLC/Thinkstock; page 50, Carlos Santa Maria/Thinkstock; page 52, George Tsartsianidis/Thinkstock; pages 54–55, stockfotoart/Shutterstock; page 56, Carsten Reisinger/Shutterstock; page 58, v.s.anandhakrishna/Shutterstock; pages 62–63, Zoonar RF/Thinkstock; page 64, Devonyu/Thinkstock; page 66, Francesco83/Shutterstock; page 69, FooTToo/Shutterstock; page 70, Jan Kratochvila/Shutterstock; pages 72–73, Keith Levit/Thinkstock; page 74, BrianAJackson/Thinkstock; pages 76–77, Sergey Peterman/Shutterstock; page 78, Olga Miltsova/Thinkstock; pages 80–81, karamysh/Shutterstock; page 82, fuyu liu/Shutterstock; page 84, Vstock LLC/Getty Images; page 85, Dalton Dingelstad/Shutterstock; pages 86–87, David Vernon/Getty Images; page 89, dam2000/Shutterstock; page 90, FotografiaBasica/Getty Images; pages 92–93, NATUREPHOTO457/Thinkstock; page 94, FotografiaBasica/Getty Images; page 96, Andrey_Kuzmin/Thinkstock; page 98, Alexandr Shirokov/Thinkstock; pages 100–101, Heike Kampe/Thinkstock; page 102, Robert Daly/Getty Images; page 103, M. Unal Ozmen/Shutterstock; page 105, eyeidea/Shutterstock; page 107, Manczurov/Shutterstock; page 108–109, Peter Booth/Getty Images; page 111, ultrapro/Thinkstock.

Published by Simple Truths, an imprint of Sourcebooks, Inc.

P.O. Box 4410, Naperville, Illinois 60567-4410

(630) 961-3900

Fax: (630) 961-2168

www.sourcebooks.com

Printed and bound in the United States of America.

WOZ 10 9 8 7 6 5 4 3 2 1

CONTENTS

THE POWER OF PERCEPTION—
WHAT DO YOU SEE?

Imagine this: you are born on Friday the 13th. What does this mean to you? Do you feel cursed or blessed? After all, this is the legendary day that inspired superstitious books and horror movies for years. Now imagine your name is Murphy, as in "Murphy's Law." You know the saying: "If anything can go wrong, it will."

Let's move on to "the terrible twos." Anyone reading this book with children can relate to the challenges of this mystical age—when fearless children challenge conventional thinking with intrepid adventures that leave parents wondering, "What???" From here, imagine you move through life with heart-shocking moments of loss and despair, dreams crushed by unexpected events. How do you take this? How do you see it? What direction do you allow it to take you?

I am all of these realities —and none of them.

I was born on Friday the 13th, my name is Murphy, and I had two near-death experiences before the age of three. I grew up reciting an "I am not worthy" mantra through the church and had many dreams dashed without notice, giving credence to my programmed belief system. I never really understood *we become what we dwell on*. We attract what we are, what we think, and what we feel day after day. Given my circumstances, it was easy to fall into a victim consciousness from time to time, a perpetual state of powerlessness. One thing simply led to another. I struggled, and with every struggle, more struggle seemed to find me.

I am not sure exactly when I **"woke up."** It was more of a gradual stage for me than a sudden awakening. Nevertheless, I learned to take each of my life circumstances and play them accordingly—like a hand of cards. Spiritually, we are dealt what we are dealt in life, with all of our best soulful interests and learning in mind. Some call this karma. It is up to us to figure out how to play the hand we have and transcend karma. If we have debts to pay, we must pay them and learn from the experience. We must live to be debt-free at the soul level. How we choose to see the world—and ourselves in the world—makes all the difference.

It took me awhile to understand this, but I apparently chose Friday the 13th as a date of fortune. Evidently, I love the name Murphy. With deeper understanding and appreciation I am now bringing new meaning to the infamous law. My early brushes with death led me to new insights on death. What an awakening! What a sense of freedom!

Join me now in this powerful, soulful book on life.

We are all co-creators. We are all blessed with an opportunity to bring greater joy and prosperity to this world. The hand we were dealt simply makes it interesting—fascinating, in fact. What an extraordinary learning opportunity we all have. **And the secret to it all is in how we perceive things.** Stop and ask yourself: How do you perceive the world? How do you perceive yourself in the world? What assumptions are you making—about yourself, your circumstances, history, heritage, genetics, family, education, religion, health, career, and everything else you experience? Now think of these perceptions and assumptions as mental programs, perhaps even viruses. What difference is this making in your life? Is your "operating system" delivering the results you really want?

We have all heard "I will believe it when I see it." Try turning this around: We see it when we believe it. We experience it when we live it in the now. We call to our existence exactly what we are thinking and feeling and believing in the moment. Contemplate this: What am I calling into my life right now? What conscious and subconscious programs am I running on right now? What mental and emotional baggage am I clinging to? Is my life half-empty, or half-full? More importantly, what is even "in the glass," and how long have I been holding on to it? **What if I chose to find and embrace the silver linings, the life lessons in disguise?**

What if I chose to let go of the baggage I have been carrying around? This choice in perception makes all the difference.

John J. Murphy

FRIDAY THE 13TH—
HALF-FULL?

WELL, THAT EXPLAINS
EVERYTHING.

When I was born on Friday the 13th, I had no knowledge of this mystical date; at least, not at the human level. After all, I was only zero years old. All I knew was I was glad to be here. It wasn't until years later that I learned that the day I was born was a day of superstition and doubt, translating into bad luck. It's right up there with ladders and black cats. People would laugh when I told them I was born on this peculiar day, and some would even say, "Well, that explains everything." I was often referred to as "hell on wheels" by teachers, coaches, friends, and relatives.

When I coupled these perceptions and beliefs with other instances in my life, I started to wonder. Could it be true? **Am I destined for hard luck and trouble?** Maybe this date has something to do with the many accidents I experienced growing up. After all, I had more stitches by the age of five than my six siblings combined. My mother now jokes that she probably should have put a doctor on retainer. Did I have something to do with the high cost of health care? I must have had something to do with childproof containers.

Looking back, I never realized that, at some level, I probably started believing in this superstition. Consciously or subconsciously, I started to learn doubt. I started to second-guess myself. I learned to be afraid. **New "programs" were developing in my mind,** and they would haunt me for years to come.

Confidence is a critical success factor in any arena, but especially in the arena of life. When we wake up in the morning, what do we believe? What do we see in the mind's eye? What do we expect? What are we calling into our experience? With every person we meet, with every task we face, with every problem we need to solve—what do we anticipate? Clearly, there are no guarantees.

Life is full of variables.
Sometimes, we get a curveball.
Sometimes, we swing and miss. But
doubt is not a welcome guest in
this equation. Doubt breeds doubt.
Is the glass half-empty, or is it half-
full? And even if it appears low, the
true champion will note, "There is still
something left." **A small flame can
light an entire room of darkness.**

John J. Murphy

EXERCISE

Think of one time in your life
when you were delivered a
curveball and you turned it into
a hit. You had your doubts
at first. You were surprised
by something unexpected,
something that set you back.
It was painful, maybe even
agonizing or humiliating.
But you worked through it and
came out stronger, wiser, and
more confident on the other side.
How does the glass look now?

"Whether you think you can
or you think you can't—
you're right."

—Henry Ford

MURPHY'S LAW

"Nothing is as easy as it looks. Everything takes longer than you expect. And if anything can go wrong, it will—at the worst possible moment."

Murphy's infamous law is often expressed with humor and lightheartedness. But what if you believed it?

What if you approached each day with this paradigm in mind?

Could it be true? Could people really have such bad luck? After all, it is referred to as a law. And what if your life experiences gave credence to this law? What if things did tend to go wrong? What would life be like if this was part of your mental programming? Rather than approaching each day with confidence and poise, you approached it with hesitation and doubt? You worried about hurting or humiliating yourself. You kept your mouth shut, procrastinated, and held back. You resisted new ideas, avoided meeting new people, and feared taking risks. You dreaded uncertainty or passed on adventures. You trapped your soul. You denied your free spirit.

With a name like Murphy, it is rare to *not* know about this law. People laugh about it all the time. They comment on it. It is published and referenced in many establishments. I grew up with it. I thought about it a lot. What if it were true? Like any "glass," the difference comes at the level of perception and belief. Is it half-full or half-empty? Do we laugh about it and dismiss it as pure fiction? Or is there some subconscious expectation that hidden within the laughter, there is truth?

What if you coupled the name Murphy with a birth date of Friday the 13th? Hmmm… Now add to that mix a high frequency of accidents and set-backs, and what might our subconscious mind be calling for? What might our habitual mind manifest into our personal reality? What self-fulfilling prophecy might we experience—time after time after time?

Could it be that our perception *becomes* our reality?

It isn't necessarily that our perception *is* reality, as many people claim. This is a very common assumption, but certainly not a fact. The Earth may appear to be flat to the individual perception, but this does not make it true. It may seem that we are standing still, but indeed the Earth is spinning at more than 1,100 miles per hour and hurling through space at more than 65,000 miles per hour. I don't see a lot of people screaming "yippee" like they do at an amusement park. It may appear that we are sitting in silence, but on a different frequency, there is music in the air—all kinds of it, along with talk radio, sports broadcasts, news reports, and

a variety of other waves. **Just because we don't hear it does not mean it is not there.** Perception can be very misleading! It is worth identifying and challenging our assumptions, especially when they limit us and hold us back.

There is plenty of evidence that what we hold to be true in the mind can manifest into evidence in the physical experience, reinforcing our belief—good or bad. In other words, we see it when we believe it! We experience it when we expect it. We find what we are looking for. We attract what we are thinking and feeling at an energetic level.

We call into our lives that which we are calling for from the heart and from the mind. We are cocreators. We ask, and it is given to us. We seek, and we find. This ancient prophecy holds true. The Law of Attraction is timeless, just, and wise. It maintains that we are eternal, spiritual beings and on an energetic level; *like frequencies attract like frequencies.* **Positive people attract positive people.** Misery loves company!

EXERCISE

Think of a time in your life when you approached an important situation or person with total confidence. You were well prepared and looked forward to the event. Perhaps it was a job interview, a speech, a presentation, a proposal, or a competition of some kind. What difference did this make? How did you go about preparing for this moment? What vision did you have in your mind's eye? What outcome did you have in mind? To what extent did you truly believe in this outcome? What lessons did you gain from the experience?

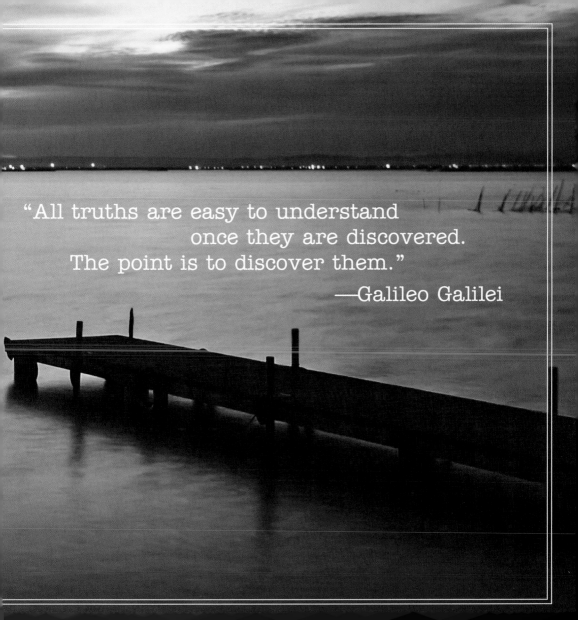

"All truths are easy to understand once they are discovered. The point is to discover them."

—Galileo Galilei

THE TERRIBLE
TWOS

I don't really know where the phrase "the terrible twos" comes from. Perhaps my mother and I had something to do with it. My understanding is that it has been around for a long time and many parents can relate to it. I know mine could, particularly when one of them drove home from church on a Sunday morning to find the other in the front yard in his underwear, shaving cream all over his face, frantically fishing me out of the bushes. I had just fallen from a second-floor window. Apparently, I was jumping on the bed with my siblings when I managed to bounce through the screen and out into the front yard. If anything can go wrong, it will—at the worst possible moment.

The good news is that I didn't kill myself and I learned I couldn't fly. Even though I was only two years old, I remember this experience like it was yesterday. When you are in mid-air without a parachute, you learn quickly and you remember the moment. **Some lessons do carry a lot of weight.** I was raced to the hospital...again. The only repair work necessary this time was the restitching of my right arm. Less than a week earlier, I had ripped open my bicep on a tree limb, requiring about fifty stitches. Friday the 13th, Murphy...hell on wheels. What was I to think?

We all make mistakes, and sometimes it may appear to be bad luck, karma, poor timing, or even someone else's fault. Surely, we find blame around every corner.

John J. Murphy

But finding blame
is no different than
viewing the glass as
half-empty.

It is representative of a victim consciousness. It is a weaker, lower-level energetic frequency that draws more of the same to the victim. As long as we hold on to this level of thinking, we manifest more examples of victimhood into our lives. We become what we dwell on. We attract what we are. If we believe we have nothing to do with our circumstances, we disempower ourselves—often without even knowing it. Most of this thinking is programmed at a *subconscious* level.

> **To move past blame, we must focus on forgiveness —one of the highest and most powerful frequencies we can reach.**

John J. Murphy

When we forgive others, regardless of the circumstances, we free ourselves. We transcend victim consciousness and elevate to higher awareness. We wake up and vibrate at a whole different energy level. **In forgiving others, we actually forgive ourselves.** We let go of the fear-based, dualistic, right–wrong ego thought system driving most human behavior, and we awaken to our true spiritual nature.

Our ability to let go of negative thoughts, denial, and resistance is our ticket to freedom. We have to let go to let flow.

I picked up a lot of baggage by the age of three. On one occasion, I decided to take some aspirin because I was not feeling well and I did not want to take my nap. Apparently, I had learned about aspirin from my parents and older siblings. I do not recall. Anyway, I climbed out of my crib, ascended the bathroom sink, found the aspirin on the top shelf of the medicine cabinet, and proceeded to take most of the bottle. As far as I was concerned, I was solving my own problem. Fortunately, my mother discovered the situation in time, rushed me to the hospital, and had my stomach pumped, and I was again given a chance to spend more time on Earth. By the age of three, there was plenty to celebrate. Despite being a Murphy born on Friday the 13th, I was still alive.

EXERCISE

Think of a time when you blamed someone else for an undesired outcome in your life. What did this accomplish? Who felt the anger? Who felt the resentment? Who experienced the grief, the pain, the regret, the despair? How did you overcome these feelings? How did you avoid turning the situation into an endless, dualistic ego battle? What enabled your freedom? Now contrast this with a time in your life when you truly forgave someone, including yourself, for undesired outcomes. How did this feel? Contemplate the difference in energy. Notice the relationship between letting go and letting flow. Forgiveness is freedom.

"Only those who will risk going too far
can possibly find out
how far one can go."

—T. S. Eliot

Affirmations and mantras (instruments of the mind) are powerful. When we recite something over and over again, we elevate it from a random thought to a programmed belief. It moves from the conscious mind to the subconscious mind, or habitual mind. At this deeper level, often hidden from our day-to-day awareness, we find our autopilot. It is the subconscious mind that multitasks and runs most of our lives.

In fact, the subconscious mind is scientifically proven to be approximately one million times more powerful in terms of processing data than the conscious mind.

It truly runs our lives *in the now* while our conscious mind is often busy processing thoughts about the past and the future. The conscious mind frequently drifts from the present moment (which is why so many people struggle with meditation), and the subconscious mind takes over. The subconscious mind has no capacity to drift from the present and think in terms of the past or future. It is always in the now.

What does this mean?
It means check your programming!

What subconscious thoughts are driving your everyday behavior and results? **What are you attracting into your life by your hidden beliefs?** What if you tell yourself consciously that the glass is half-full, but your subconscious programming sees it as half-empty? What if you are telling yourself you can do it, but your hidden, far more powerful belief system is saying you can't? Is it any wonder that willpower so often fails to overcome the habitual mind?

John J. Murphy

The challenge we all face is that we don't really know what we think at the subconscious level. It is below consciousness. It is hidden. It is so common to us that we do not see the box. When someone says, "Think outside the box," we wonder, "What box?" We spend our lives trying to solve problems within the box when it is actually the box—the paradigm, the mental model, the belief system—that *is* the problem. It is tough to see a paradigm when we are in one.

I grew up going to church every Sunday, if not every day, reciting "I am not worthy." The words became so familiar, I often just said them without even thinking or contemplating their meaning at all.

It wasn't until later in life that **I learned to challenge assumptions** like these and search for deeper understanding. Where are these interpretations coming from, and why? What impact are they having on my life and the lives of others? Is there a relationship between my name, my birth date, my current outcomes, and these beliefs? What we sow is what we reap! What happens when an unworthy, unlucky, superstitious, accident-prone person steps up to the plate of life? Don't answer that.

It all depends on how you look at it.

EXERCISE

Think of an affirmation or mantra
you have recited or believed all
of your life. What impact has this
had on your outcomes?
What might change if you
believed something entirely
different? How would you feel
without these limiting thoughts
and beliefs? Consider many of
the norms you may have grown
up with, such as blame, revenge,
control, and the many "dos"and
"don'ts" we are programmed with.

"A man's mind stretched
    to a new idea never goes back
to its original dimensions."
    —Oliver Wendell Holmes, Sr.

THE DARK
AGES

One of my deepest passions growing up was sports. I excelled in several different sports, and this kept me motivated and grounded. It might have been easy to throw in the towel after so many mishaps if I didn't have something I loved to do every day. **We all need a light at the end of a dark tunnel.** It gives us hope.

Athletics gave me a sense of purpose. They also helped me build confidence, friendships, and stamina. **Perhaps I was inspired at some level to confront the limiting beliefs and doubts I had buried away beneath the surface.** Despite appearing confident on the surface, I had insecurity lurking about, no doubt remnants from my tumultuous past.

Swimming was my dominant sport as a child, but it was football that captured my imagination and attention in my teens. I wallpapered my room with pictures and posters of great players and invested countless hours playing catch with my brothers and friends. By my sophomore year in high school, I was a top contender for the quarterback position and my confidence was building. It was then that I discovered I had a hernia and was essentially out for the season. At that time, a hernia repair required six days in the hospital and a very long recovery. More time in the hospital. More stitches. More bad news. If anything can go wrong, it will—at the worst possible moment. I am not worthy.

I had the hernia repaired, diligently and delicately returned to practice, and by season's end, I got in one game. There was still light at the end of the tunnel. For the next two years, I worked hard to develop my skills and to compete for a starting position. Losing this pivotal year of experience at age fifteen did not help my chances, but I was not going to give up. **Passion has power.** At age sixteen, our team won the state championship in Michigan, and I was elected captain for my senior year.

For many years to come, **I wondered what triggered the next big challenge in life.** Was it my subconscious, limiting beliefs? Was it karma? Was there some unpaid debt I had yet to pay? I really didn't know. Maybe it was just bad luck. But when I was being rushed to the hospital at age seventeen after severely injuring my foot with a lawn mower, I wanted to scream. In fact, I did scream. What did I do to deserve this? Why me? Why now? Again, my dreams were dashed. Again, I screwed up. Again, my life went dark. The glass? It seemed to be cracked and leaking at this point.

In retrospect, I see now why this happened. It was meant to. It happened because it happened. It was to be part of my life lesson, my soul development, my test of character. What would I do now? **How would I respond when there didn't appear to be anything in the glass at all?** Who could help? How? The surgeon said my football days were over. Should I hang up the cleats and return to swimming? What about some of the other sports I enjoyed? There has to be some hope. There has to be something left in the glass.

I received a gift from my grandfather, a book on courage. In this book, there was a very inspiring story about Rocky Bleier, a four-time Super Bowl winner who had severely damaged his leg and foot while fighting in Vietnam. Despite the odds, Rocky returned to football and stepped up as a champion. That's all I needed to read. The glass had light in it—the stuff the universe is made of. Two years later, I was playing football for the University of Notre Dame. Mind over matter is no joke. Miracles do happen. **Our perception becomes our reality.** My awakening continued.

EXERCISE

Think of a time when you were set back. Identify a major challenge or adverse experience you faced. How did you view this experience at the time? How do you view it now? Do you see it any differently? Was this a blessing in disguise? What did you learn from it? Have you learned to use it to your advantage? Has the experience made you stronger? If not, try looking at it a different way. We are not given problems we cannot solve. At a spiritual level, every challenge we face has positive consequences. Do you see them?

CROSSROADS

Eighteen months into my first job out of college, I came to a crossroads. I discovered that the finance degree I earned from Notre Dame and **the career path I selected was not what I really wanted**. I made a mistake—again—or so it seemed.

I was working in the corporate headquarters for a very large company based in Chicago at the time and loving my life—outside of work. My initial training was interesting and exciting, but after it was over, I started feeling complacent and underutilized. With every day that went by, the boredom grew. I felt weary during the day, like the administrative work was sucking the life out of me. I needed more. **I needed a greater challenge.** After coming from a very assertive learning culture like Notre Dame and playing football in a very competitive environment, I wanted action and interaction. This work culture felt slow and isolating to me.

How often have you made good progress down a path, only to discover that you are heading in the wrong direction? What do you do now? Grin and bear it? Turn around? Ask for directions? What if you have a lot invested in the direction you are going? And what if you are doing really well at the job or relationship? What if you are being rewarded well for it? Does that change your mind?

This was a crossroads for me: I had a lot invested in this direction, and I was doing very well at it. I loved Chicago and had made many good friends there. I just wasn't excited and inspired by what I was doing. It was like I was a fish out of water: motivated to stay alive, but not really comfortable with the environment.
I needed a change.

My first option was to talk with my boss about the situation and the possibility of making a transition to another part of the company, perhaps sales. She advised me to talk with the human resources department. I made an appointment with HR and was informed that I could not make any kind of transition outside of my department for another year. I had to stay put. This seemed like a very long stoplight.

I gave this crossroad a lot of thought and, in the end, decided to make a change. Some might say I backed up a bit, taking a cut in pay to accept a position in human resources with another company, but it didn't matter to me.

I needed work that was good for my soul. I wanted to feel inspired, creative, and purposeful every day. The job in HR was a better fit for me. Besides, I made up the pay difference within a year and things blossomed even more after that.

Considering that I am now writing books, consulting with companies around the world, teaching classes, and giving speeches, it is probably obvious that I have come to many crossroads in my life. I find these situations interesting and helpful. They challenge us to think about who we are and what we really want—beyond the intellectual level. What do our hearts and souls call for? What do we feel passionate about? **What really inspires us?** We are all different, and we have to find a path that suits us well. I know my friend Jim did. Jim and I were fellow recruits coming into the same company in Chicago in 1982 from two different universities. I chose my path to leave the company and explore other avenues. Jim stayed and went on to serve as the company's president in Europe and then Asia. Recently, we had dinner together in Shanghai, and we shared life stories about our countless adventures—two different paths leading to the same place. Pay attention. **It is the journey that matters most.**

EXERCISE

Identify a crossroad in your life, past or present. What is troubling you? Carefully identify the various options you have. Recognize that you have free choice. You always have options. For each option, list the reason why you should choose this option. Write them down. Now list all the reasons why you should not choose each option. What are the forces for and against each? Listen to your heart, not just your head. What feels most inspiring? Pay close attention to the culture and environment you are in. Now identify the barriers to this option and plan accordingly. Write down the "countermeasures" you will use to overcome the obstacles in your way. Use the crossroads in your life to clarify focus, align your priorities, and mobilize commitment.

"The field is the sole governing agency of the particle."

—Albert Einstein

FIRED
OR FREED?

In 1988, I was set free. Put another way, I was fired. The company I was working for had been acquired by a large European company, and my position was no longer needed. At first, the news came as a bit of a shock. The timing wasn't exactly good. My wife was pregnant with our second child, and we had very little in savings. An echo sounded off in my head: "If anything can go wrong, it will—at the worst possible moment."

In many respects, **this was another crossroad in life.** I could continue to go straight and extend my career as a human resources director, or I could consider alternatives. I really liked my job at the time, and the cultural transformation we were making at our U.S. companies was quite progressive. We even made the national news. Nevertheless, I had an intuitive calling to teach, consult, and explore life further.

Losing something or someone you value is not easy. It feels as if part of your human identity has been ripped away. You can feel exposed, vulnerable, perhaps even humiliated. A form of habit or comfort has suddenly disappeared, and you are forced to adapt. You have to pull yourself together and **step up to the new challenge,** one way or another. Again, you find yourself peering into the mystical glass of life. What is in this glass? How much is there? What can I do with it?

For me, this glass didn't appear to have a whole lot of substance in it.

There was certainly very little money and savings in it. My résumé was nothing exceptional. I didn't have a master's degree or a PhD. What now? *Should* I start doubting myself? *Should* I have stayed with my original job back in Chicago? *Should* I have gone back to school? *Should* I have changed my name? How depressing to look at it this way!

After careful thought and contemplation, I decided to not *should* myself. I had seen this glass before, seemingly empty. I had experienced unexpected loss and grief. I knew the routine. I was simply facing another test of character and strength, **an opportunity to rise from the ashes.** Once again, the greatest obstacle to joy and prosperity was me and how I looked at things.

Look again at what appears to be an empty glass and observe the light. Bear witness to the photons, the stuff the universe is made of. They are always there, always present. Sometimes, people forget this. We get so hung up on physical substance that we forget what is behind it all. We get so attached to temporary things that we forget they are temporary. As a result, we live in subconscious fear of losing that which is temporary, including the very people we care about most. Spiritually, the only things that really matter are those that are *not* temporary—the unconditional love, forgiveness, compassion, health, and well-being of the soul. We must learn to care for the soul. **The more we give of what is truly real, the more we have of it to give!**

I never realized how afraid I was until I lost the things— and people—I was most afraid of losing. Adversity can be very revealing. Yet, when we let go of the fear and insecurity holding us back and allow the life force to flow through us as it is meant to, **we begin to see the world very differently.** In this case, I saw

an opportunity to pursue a whole new career, an opportunity to drop the baggage, spread my wings and fly even higher. It was then that I incorporated my company and became a child again—fearless, innovative, and free. I look back now with deep gratitude. I was imprisoned, and I didn't even know it.

EXERCISE

Think of a time in your life when you suddenly lost something you valued deeply—a job, a relationship, or an asset of some kind. What did you think? How did you feel? How did you see the situation? Did you play victim or champion? Did you hold on to these feelings of loss and despair, or let them go? Take time now to imagine how you might feel if you let go of all of the thoughts bringing you down. Remember, a thought triggers a feeling. If you want to feel free, you have to release the thoughts and beliefs trapping you.

"There is no scarcity of the things that matter most—like love and forgiveness. The more we give, the more we have to give."

—John J. Murphy

LOST OR
LOVED?

On my birthday in 1999, I learned that my father was diagnosed with cancer. He and my mother called to wish me a happy day, then disclosed the news that quickly changed the mood. My first reaction was shock. How could this be? My father seemed so strong and healthy. Then, I switched into my problem-solving mode. What is the cause of this? What do we do now? How do we solve this problem? It wasn't until much later that **I learned a deeper truth**—fear and stress in circumstances like this only make matters worse.

For the next eleven months, my father "fought the fight," and I was among the many people cheering him on. Right to the end, we battled this disease, becoming more dis-at-ease with each blow. Each day delivered what we were looking for—a fight! We simply didn't realize that *what we resist, we make stronger.* Fear accelerates illness. Doubt weakens the immune system. Cells become vulnerable with anxiety and stress. **We become what we dwell on.** If we dwell on illness, we attract it into our lives. This is the Law of Attraction.

Ten years after my father died, I was attending a health conference in California when I met a woman who shared an interesting story with me. In 1999, she was diagnosed with terminal cancer. After receiving a variety of traditional cancer-fighting techniques, she was sent home to die. She was miserable. A friend suggested she try a holistic health center in West Palm Beach, Florida. With little to lose, she stopped fighting and started loving. **She learned how to see the glass as half-full,** despite what other professionals and naysayers told her. She learned to let go and let flow. Within months, she was cancer-free.

I was intrigued by this story for several reasons. One, this woman has now lived a healthy and productive life for more than ten years without any hint of cancer. Two, my father died in West Palm Beach without any knowledge of this alternative—very close by. Three, I had just written a book on how to **"let go and let flow."**

A powerful synchronicity was presenting itself. Perhaps there was more I could do to share healthy alternatives for people suffering. My father was not lost. He was helping me. He was guiding me spiritually to live, learn, and love.

One of the books I wrote during this time is called *Beyond Doubt: Four Steps to Inner Peace.* The four steps are *Let Be, Let Go, Let See, and Let Flow.* To transcend doubt and fear-based, competitive ego-thinking, **we have to accept what *is* and let go** of any denial, resistance, bitter judgment, or criticism. Rather than cling to the worry, stress, and anxiety that weakens us, we have to let it go. For many, this is counterintuitive. **We tend to cling to the very things weighing us down,** including serious diseases, by focusing our attention on them. Fortunately, when we release these toxic thoughts and feelings, we begin to see the world very differently. And when we "let see," we allow healthy, spiritual flow into our lives. **This flow translates into a sense of deep inner peace,** timelessness, fearlessness, innovation, and peak productivity. Many successful professionals refer to this as "the zone." It is where true emotional intelligence, wisdom, and genius reside. It is a field beyond right and wrong, a place the mystics call nirvana or heaven.

When we gain from a loss, there is no loss. We are simply experiencing the perfect yin-yang balance of the universe. **This contrast is what makes life interesting,** the perfect playing field for the soul. We cannot know *up* without knowing *down*. We cannot know *light* without knowing *dark*. The amount is irrelevant. It is what is in the glass and how long we hold on to it that matters.

John J. Murphy

EXERCISE

Take note of your attractions and aversions. What are the things and who are the people you are most attracted to in life? Who and what do you want to avoid? How attached to these thoughts are you? Does the thought of losing any of this worry you? Are you living life in fear? How would you feel without these thoughts? What would life be like if you simply loved and appreciated the people and experiences you have in life—without attachment or aversion? Letting go does not mean giving up. It is not a sign of weakness. Rather, it is a sign of great wisdom and strength. Let go to let flow!

"Out beyond ideas of wrongdoing
and rightdoing, there is a field.
I will meet you there."
—Jalal ad-Din Rumi

DIVORCED OR
DELIVERED?

In 2010, my wife filed for divorce. Again, I felt shocked. It was like getting punched in the stomach unexpectedly. Was this Friday the 13th and Murphy's Law coming back to haunt me? Should I start "should-ing" myself? How could this be after twenty-six years together? How could this be with four wonderful children together?

What did I do to deserve this?

For several months, I asked her to reconsider, unaware that I was being delivered from subconscious peril. Our relationship was no longer healthy and productive. We were moving in two different directions and losing our synergy. Temptations to blame each other arose and feelings of defensiveness, rationalization, and competitiveness surfaced. I remember thinking: *How do I defend myself? How do I prove that I am right? How do I win this battle?* Then I realized—**these were thoughts I needed to let go.**

The truth is, I didn't even know where to start. I had no understanding or knowledge about divorce. All I knew is that I never expected one. Therefore, I never put much time and energy into learning more about it—until I had to! Now I had to learn.

Again, the glass was looking pretty empty.

I had no knowledge. I had no money stashed away. We were just coming out of the worst economic recession in my lifetime, and it wreaked havoc on my business and personal finances. In fact, we were in quite a bit of debt. The tunnel was dark.

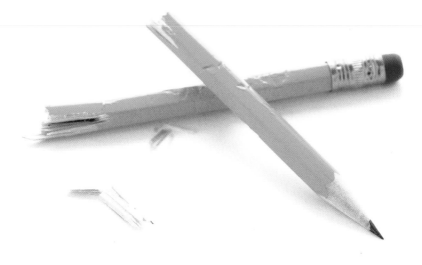

When I first received the news,

I sat quietly in wonder,
contemplating the situation.

The house was empty, and I had time to myself. Somewhere between tears of sorrow and tears of joy, reminiscing on the past twenty-six years, I found myself searching the Internet for guidance on how to respond. Surely, there had to be some wise advice available. Within minutes, I found a great resource on how to handle this exact situation. Thank God for miracles.

The first suggestion was exactly the *opposite* of what I thought I had to do—do *not* hire a lawyer. The reasoning was simple. **Try to resolve the situation peacefully and save yourself a lot of time and money.** I found this advice peculiar, especially since I did not know anything about the divorce process or law. The book continued to share very practical ideas and insights on how to navigate the laws effectively and solve the problem rationally. I read the entire book in two days.

As a consultant training thousands of people all over the world, I find great value in delivering honest, intelligent, and practical advice. People appreciate it. I know I do. **Often, we can take one problem and turn it into several more without wise counsel.** We tend to complicate the simple and add when we should be subtracting. I was ready to do the same thing with my divorce—complicate it and turn it into multiple other problems.

Instead, **I chose the road less traveled** and proposed to work in peace with my wife. She agreed, despite her legal counsel, and we settled in peace. We even drove to the courthouse together and had lunch afterward. To this day, I love my ex-wife and wish her the very best. We simply came to a fork in the mystical road of life and wanted different directions. **The power of perception is just that—powerful!**

Looking back, I do not wish divorce on anyone. It was a dark, difficult, challenging time for me. I felt lost and betrayed at times. I was hurt and suffering. Nonetheless, **I found light at the end of the tunnel and a glass with something left in it to work with.** Years later, this positive attitude and optimistic approach to life have worked wonders for both of us. We have moved on as friends with many great memories together.

EXERCISE

Identify a difficult or challenging relationship in your life. What thoughts do you hold to be true about this person and his or her intentions? How certain are you about these thoughts? Are they facts or assumptions? How do you know? How do you feel as a result of these thoughts? What alternatives exist? What assumptions are *you* making? Could it be that your partner or friend is hurting or suffering in some way? People who are in pain—consciously or subconsciously—can say and do things that are harmful. Can you see past this? Can you find a silver lining? Ignorance is the root cause to most pain and suffering. We often "know not what we do." Use forgiveness to let go of negative thoughts and feelings. It is our salvation.

"Life shrinks or expands
in proportion to one's courage."
—Anaïs Nin

THE ROAD
LESS TRAVELED

A lot of people just want to fit in. We value community and a sense of belonging. We consider it safe. We may even consider it part of our identity after a while, thinking we are what we are labeled—a mom, a doctor, a lawyer, a vice president, a sales rep, a teacher. **We grow up being taught to follow the norms.** Go to school. Get a good job. Play by the numbers. Do as you are told. Listen to the experts. Stay within the lines. Avoid risk. Hold tight to what you have. Save for a rainy day. Protect yourself. Try not to get hurt. Be loyal. Be on time. Work hard. Finish what you start. Follow these rules and you will be successful. **You will be happy.**

I grew up this way, always planning somehow for another day. In some ways, I was being taught that success and happiness are somewhere in the future, after the next degree or promotion. I appreciate the love and concern teachers, parents, and professionals have when they offer this advice. It can be very helpful. It can also guarantee you nothing. **The only time that ever matters is right now.** Are we feeling happy and successful right now?

Life is not a cookbook. While some ingredients can prove to be very useful, **uncertainty is the only thing that is actually certain.** We are wise to weigh our options and be prepared to improvise. I liken this to a quarterback walking up to the line of scrimmage after calling a play that is expected to advance the team. The defense suddenly shifts, and we are forced to scramble. We have to adapt—quickly! Welcome to life, the perfect playing ground for souls in development, the perfect "school" for us to awaken.

When I was facing my painful divorce, I knew one thing: I could handle it. I had been down a similar path earlier in life, when I lost my father to cancer. In fact, each time painful losses happened in my life, I was able to handle it. Each loss blessed me with a silver lining, a lesson about myself and a lesson about life. Now when I see a glass "half-full," I smile to myself. Maybe this is just perfect. **Maybe the amount in the glass is all**

we need right now. Appreciate that! Maybe we only need half a glass. Maybe we don't need any at all, and half is more than enough. **Maybe the half is so concentrated or nutritious that it can feed a flock indefinitely.** Or maybe the glass itself is the problem and the amount inside it is irrelevant. It doesn't really help to solve problems within a "box" when the box (or paradigm) is the problem.

We can be so quick to criticize and judge. We can fall into temptation without a second thought. If I have learned anything at all, it is that **with each curse there is a blessing.** Friday the 13th has become a day of joy and celebration for me. My name has become synonymous for many as a name associated with inspiration and success. The trials and tribulations of growing up with multiple injuries and losses have strengthened me. In fact, these experiences have given me great confidence. They have made me wiser and more effective as a teacher, a writer, and a consultant. Indeed, I could not be where I am today, doing what I am doing, without these amazing life experiences. The only place I might otherwise be is at a dead-end, going around in circles, simply because I believed the glass was half-empty and I was destined for doom.

Like many people, I was given plenty of chances to adopt a line of pessimistic thinking, but I chose a different road. I listened to the medical experts when they told me I could never play football again, and then I chose to play anyway. That led me to Notre Dame, tapping a sign that reads **"Play like a champion today."** I listened to my former boss when he said I would never amount to anything as a writer, and then I challenged that assumption. This is my eighteenth published book. I listened to trusted people when they advised that I needed a lawyer to handle my divorce. I then resolved it myself with my wife and her lawyer—peacefully.

Some people might call this stubborn. I like to think of it as vigilance. **Be vigilant about what you choose to see in this world.** Recognize and respect the power of perception. There is a perfect balance of yin and yang, dark and light, feminine and masculine. Look carefully and insist on the positive. It is always there, sometimes hidden or revealed later in life. But make no mistake: your perception becomes your reality. Knowing this makes all the difference!

EXERCISE

Think of a time in your life when you were given what appeared to be "bad news." Perhaps someone told you that you couldn't or shouldn't do something your heart desired. Maybe you had one of your dreams dashed without warning. Maybe you lost something or someone very valuable to you. Now identify some of the "positive" outcomes from that seemingly "negative" event. Contemplate this carefully and patiently. Did you find a way to turn a loss into a win? Did you respond with hope and promise and conviction? Did you find something inside or outside the glass that helped?

"Mistakes are the portals
of discovery."
—James Joyce

CONCLUSION:
HALF-FULL OF WHAT?

Quantity can be quite misleading. For example, when we adopt a "bigger is better" paradigm, we risk living life as if there is never enough. We find ourselves always searching for more. Consciously and subconsciously, this translates into a "lack" mentality, which leaves us feeling unsatisfied soon after the honeymoon is over. We have temporary moments of pride and accomplishment, and then the ego kicks back in, saying we need more. The grass is greener somewhere else. We are incomplete until we get there.

A paradigm is a mental model based on unquestioned assumptions and beliefs. It is the "box" we live in, often without knowing it. We hold paradigms to be true even when there is no factual data to back them up. We just believe it, trust it, and live our lives accordingly. We adopt certain habits, customs, patterns, and practices based on these mental "programs." They exist at home and at work, virtually everywhere we go. We fight wars over them. We argue politics over them. We raise children with them. We eat at certain times of day. We eat food that is marketed as healthy (and often is quite the opposite).

We think that we have to work hard to be successful. We assume that more academic degrees means we are smarter and will help us achieve more wealth. We trust certain media as the truth. We live in paradigms about race, religion, nationality, genetics, heritage, education, family, medicine, law, relationships, love, and countless other belief systems.

And then we do the best we can within the belief (or glass) to live a healthy and happy life.

We live *inside* the glass (a paradigm itself) and assume that more is better (a paradigm within a paradigm). We are trained to think in terms of scarcity—that there is not enough for all, that in order to win someone has to lose, that the survival of the fittest rules the game. We then seek ways to win within a perpetual win-lose system. We divide and conquer. We value competition over cooperation. We debate religion and politics as if one is right and the other is wrong. We add complexity to the system—to all our systems—by being fearful and resistant. We find ways to fill the glass with more activity, more confusion, more barriers, and more defenses.

John J. Murphy

Happiness
NEXT EXIT ↗

I believe there is life outside the glass,
and it is what we see inside the glass
that makes the difference.

This means we have to look deep within ourselves, beyond the resistant and insecure ego, to our true spiritual, fearless nature. We have extraordinary capacity to create, explore, and innovate, but we hold ourselves back. We simply do not know what we do not know. The glass is our own self-limiting container. It holds what we believe to be true and empowers us or limits us from there. It is not the amount that matters most; it is the substance—the perceptions and beliefs we hold in mind. One truly sacred, spiritual insight can change everything. Forgiving one person can set us free. Forgiving ourselves can be equally as empowering. **Letting go of limiting beliefs and harmful habits can free up more time and space for life itself.** There is wisdom in emptiness and release. It is where miracles reveal themselves. We have to let go to let flow. A full glass can accept no more. People who are "full of themselves" limit themselves. We are free when we release the perceptions holding us captive.

So is the glass half-full or half-empty?

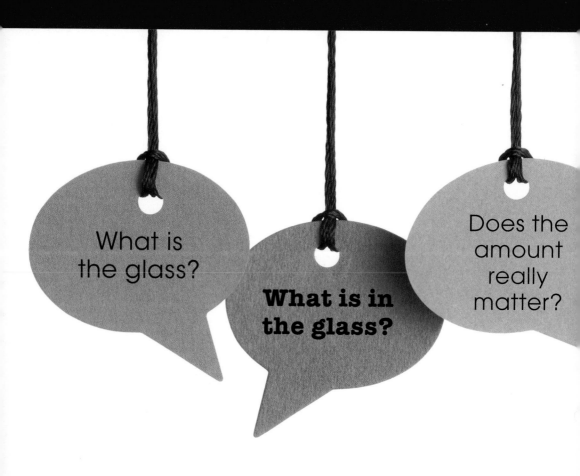

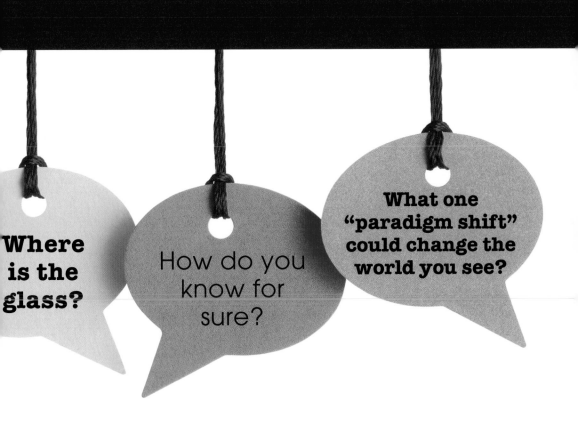

Change your perceptions, and you change your reality.

About the Author

John J. Murphy is an award-winning author, speaker, and management consultant. Drawing on a diverse collection of team experiences as a corporate manager, consultant, and collegiate quarterback, John has appeared on more than four hundred radio and television stations, and his work has been featured in over fifty newspapers nationwide.

As founder and president of Venture Management Consultants, **www.venturemanagementconsultants.com**, John specializes in creating high-performance team environments, teaching leadership and team development, and leading global rapid improvement events. He has trained thousands of "change agents" from more than fifty countries and helped some of the world's leading organizations design and implement positive change.

John is a critically acclaimed author and sought-after speaker. Among his other books are *Zentrepreneur: Get Out of the Way and Lead—Create a Culture of Innovation and Fearlessness*; *Pulling Together: 10 Rules for High Performance Teams*; *Beyond Doubt: Four Steps to Inner Peace*; *Reinvent Yourself: A Lesson in Personal Leadership*; *Agent of Change: Leading a Cultural Revolution*; *Sage Leadership: Awakening the Spirit in Work*; *The Eight Disciplines: An Enticing Look into Your Personality*; *Habits Die Hard: 10 Steps to Building Successful Habits*; *Leading with Passion: 10 Essentials for Inspiring Others*; and *The How of Wow: Secrets Behind World Class Service*.

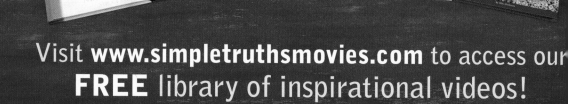